Crypto Clarity

Demystifying Cryptocurrency for Everyday Investors

Arthur Crandon LL.B (Hons) M.A.

Introduction

Why write this book?

Cryptocurrency has emerged as one of the most transformative financial innovations of the 21st century. Whether you've heard about bitcoin reaching jaw-dropping prices or seen headlines about investors becoming overnight millionaires, it's impossible to ignore the buzz surrounding this digital revolution. But for many, cryptocurrency remains shrouded in mystery, confusion, and skepticism.

This book exists to change that.

The rise of cryptocurrency signals a fundamental shift in how we think about money, investments, and financial freedom. At its core, crypto challenges traditional finance systems that have existed for centuries—systems often plagued by inefficiencies, fees, and barriers to entry. Cryptocurrency, powered by blockchain technology, introduces a decentralized, digital alternative where individuals—not banks or governments—hold greater control over their wealth.

But with opportunity comes uncertainty.

For the average person, cryptocurrency feels daunting. Maybe you've heard conflicting opinions:

- "bitcoin is the future!

- "it's a bubble that will burst!"

- "crypto is only for tech geeks or criminals!"

These misconceptions and fears stop many everyday investors from taking that first step. Perhaps you've already thought:

- *What even is cryptocurrency, and why does it matter?*

- *Is it safe to invest? Won't i lose all my money?*

- *How can I tell the difference between legitimate opportunities and scams?*

I wrote this book because I believe everyone—regardless of age, technical expertise, or investment background—should have access to clear, practical information about cryptocurrency. You don't need to be a financial expert or tech whiz to understand how this works or to invest wisely.

This book is for you: the curious, everyday person looking for clarity, confidence, and the tools to make informed decisions.

Whether you're a complete beginner or someone who has dabbled in crypto but still feels overwhelmed, you'll find step-by-step guidance, real-world examples, and simple explanations of even the most complex concepts. My goal is not to sell you on cryptocurrency but to empower you with the knowledge to decide for yourself:

- *Is crypto right for me?*
- *How can I minimize risks and maximize potential rewards?*

How to use this book

Imagine this book as a roadmap, guiding you from **crypto confusion** to **crypto confidence**. It's written with simplicity and practicality in mind, broken down into clear sections so you can learn at your own pace.

Here's what you'll discover:

1. **Foundations first**: before diving into charts, coins, and investments, we'll start with the basics. You'll learn what cryptocurrency is, how it works, and why it's valuable. Think of it as learning to crawl before you walk.

    - For example: have you heard the word *blockchain* but still have no clue what it is? We'll demystify it with relatable analogies, like imagining a secure digital ledger that everyone can see but no one can tamper with.

2. **Getting practical**: next, you'll learn exactly how to start—how to buy cryptocurrency, where to store it safely, and how to protect yourself from common mistakes. You'll see real examples of how others have successfully entered the market, and even stories of those who fell for scams (so you won't make the same errors).

3. **Investment strategies**: I'll introduce strategies that everyday people use to invest responsibly. For instance, did you know you can start investing as little as $10

using a method called *dollar-cost averaging*? No need to risk your life savings or "bet it all" on the next big coin.

4. **Real-world applications**: beyond investing, you'll see how cryptocurrency is already being used in the real world—whether it's in online payments, international remittances, or digital art through nfts. You'll hear success stories from businesses, governments, and individuals using crypto to improve their lives.

5. **Looking ahead**: finally, we'll explore the future of cryptocurrency—emerging trends, risks to watch, and what role it might play in your financial journey.

Here's the best part: you don't need to read this book cover-to-cover in one sitting. Each chapter is designed as a standalone guide. Whether you want to focus on buying your first crypto, understanding investment risks, or exploring passive income opportunities like staking, you can jump to the section that matters most to you right now.

Example of what you'll learn

To give you a glimpse of what's ahead, let me share a quick analogy:

Imagine the **internet in the 1990s**. Back then, most people didn't understand what it was. Terms like "email," "web pages," and "search engines" sounded foreign. Many dismissed the internet as a fad, while others saw its potential and seized the opportunity. Fast forward to today, and the internet has transformed every aspect of our lives.

Cryptocurrency in 2024 is like the internet in 1995—full of potential, but still misunderstood. Just like learning to send your first email or browse a website back then, understanding crypto starts with small, achievable steps. This book will help you take those steps, starting with the basics and building up to more advanced concepts.

By the time you finish, you'll know how to:
- Safely purchase and store cryptocurrency.
- Avoid scams and common pitfalls.
- Build a crypto portfolio suited to your financial goals.
- Explore ways to earn passive income from crypto.

Most importantly, you'll understand how cryptocurrency fits into your financial future—without fear, confusion, or overwhelm.

A word of encouragement

As you begin this journey, know that you are not alone. Every successful crypto investor started where you are right now: curious but unsure. This book is designed to take you by the hand, simplify the complex, and give you the tools to act confidently.

You don't need to become a blockchain developer or spend hours glued to trading charts. What you do need is clarity, common sense, and a willingness to learn—qualities you already have just by picking up this book.

So, are you ready to unlock the potential of cryptocurrency? Let's dive in and demystify this exciting new world—together.

CONTENTS

	Acknowledgments	i
1	What is Cryptocurrency?	1
2	Blockchain Technology made simple	11
3	Types of Cryptocurrencies	19
4	How to buy and sell Crypto currencies	29
5	Risk and Reward	39
6	Building a Crypto portfolio	49
7	The Art of Timing	59
8	Staking, Lending, and Earning yield	69
9	Regulation and Taxation	79
10	Change	89
11	Emerging Trends	99
12	Becoming a Savvy Investor	111
13	Conclusion	121

Not all cryptocurrencies are created equal. While many people think of cryptocurrency as a single concept—like bitcoin—the truth is the crypto space is incredibly diverse, with different types of coins serving different purposes. This chapter breaks down the key categories, provides examples of popular cryptocurrencies, and introduces you to the fascinating world of altcoins.

CHAPTER 1: WHAT IS CRYPTOCURRENCY?

DEFINING CRYPTOCURRENCY

At its core, cryptocurrency is a digital or virtual form of money that uses cryptography—a highly secure method of encrypting data—to ensure that transactions are safe and verifiable. Unlike the cash in your wallet or the balance in your bank account, cryptocurrency doesn't exist in physical form or rely on a central authority like a bank or government. Instead, it operates on decentralized networks, most commonly powered by blockchain technology.

Let's break that down:

- A **cryptocurrency** is essentially a **digital asset**. Think of it as owning a secure, tamper-proof file that represents value.

- These assets are secured using **cryptographic algorithms**, making them almost impossible to counterfeit or manipulate.

Examples to picture it:

1. **Bitcoin**: the first and most well-known cryptocurrency, often called "digital gold." It was created in 2009 as a response to the 2008 financial crisis. Bitcoin operates on a decentralized network, allowing people to send money directly to each other without a middleman.

2. **Ethereum**: another popular cryptocurrency, but with added functionality. Beyond being a digital currency, ethereum allows developers to create "smart contracts" (self-executing agreements) and decentralized applications (dapps).

3. **Emerging coins**: cryptocurrencies like solana and polkadot offer faster transactions or unique features, while meme coins like dogecoin bring humor into the market, even though their utility is limited.

Why cryptocurrency matters

Cryptocurrency isn't just a new way to hold or move money—it represents a shift in financial power and possibility.

1. **Decentralization and freedom from traditional banking** unlike traditional money systems, cryptocurrencies operate without banks or governments acting as gatekeepers. This means:

- **No middlemen:** when you send money to someone using bitcoin, the transaction happens directly, peer-to-peer, without needing a bank to process it.

- **Global access:** crypto is borderless. Whether you're in new york or nairobi, you can send funds instantly, often at a fraction of the cost of traditional systems like wire transfers.

- **Empowerment:** in countries with unstable economies or corrupt governments, cryptocurrency offers people a way to preserve and control their wealth without relying on volatile local currencies.

Example:

imagine you're a freelancer working with clients overseas. With traditional banking, you might wait days for a wire transfer, pay high fees, and deal with unfavorable exchange rates. With cryptocurrency, you could receive payment almost instantly, directly to your digital wallet, and at a lower cost.

2. **Use cases beyond money**
   while bitcoin started as "digital cash," cryptocurrencies have expanded their use cases to include:

- **Payments:** platforms like bitpay and companies like tesla (temporarily) accept bitcoin for goods and services.

- **Investments:** people buy cryptocurrencies like bitcoin or ethereum as digital assets, hoping their value will increase over time.

- **Innovation:** technologies like decentralized finance (defi) allow users to earn interest, borrow, or lend money without traditional banks. Nfts (non-fungible tokens) are transforming how we think about digital art and ownership.

Cryptocurrency isn't just a passing trend—it's a tool reshaping how we save, spend, and invest.

Comparison with traditional assets

To understand cryptocurrency, it's essential to compare it with something we all know: **fiat money**, or the traditional currencies we use every day, like dollars, euros, or pesos.

1. **Fiat money: strengths and weaknesses**
   fiat currencies are government-issued and backed by trust in that government rather than physical commodities like gold. For example, the us dollar is valuable because people trust the us government and economy.

- **Strengths of fiat money:**
-
  - **Stability:** fiat currencies are generally stable and predictable (though this can vary depending on the country).

  - **Universal acceptance:** you can use dollars to pay for nearly anything.

- **Legal tender:** governments mandate the use of fiat money for debts, taxes, and trade.

- **Weaknesses of fiat money:**

    - **Inflation:** central banks can print more money, diluting its value over time. For instance, the us dollar has lost 96% of its purchasing power since 1913 due to inflation.

    - **Lack of privacy:** digital fiat transactions are recorded and monitored by banks and governments.

    - **Exclusivity:** billions of people globally lack access to traditional banking systems, excluding them from the financial world.

Example of weakness:

in countries like venezuela, hyperinflation has rendered the local currency nearly worthless, forcing citizens to turn to alternatives like bitcoin to preserve their savings.

2. Cryptocurrency: strengths and weaknesses

cryptocurrencies address many of fiat money's weaknesses while introducing new challenges of their own.

- **Strengths of cryptocurrency:**

    - **Decentralization:** no central authority can manipulate the supply or control your funds.

    - **Limited supply:** many cryptocurrencies, like bitcoin, have a capped supply, making them immune to inflation caused by overprinting.

    - **Transparency:** blockchain technology records every transaction in a public ledger, ensuring accountability.

    - **Global access:** anyone with an internet connection can own and trade cryptocurrency.

- **Weaknesses of cryptocurrency:**

    - **Volatility:** prices can fluctuate wildly, leading to potential losses. For instance, bitcoin dropped from $69,000 in 2021 to $16,000 in 2022 before recovering.

    - **Complexity:** the learning curve is steep for newcomers, with terms like "blockchain" and "hash rates" feeling like a foreign language.

    - **Security risks:** while the blockchain is secure, scams, hacks, and user errors (like losing your private key) can lead to lost funds.

Fiat money vs. Cryptocurrency: a quick comparison

Feature	Fiat money	Cryptocurrency
Control	Centralized (governments, banks)	Decentralized (peer-to-peer)
Inflation	Unlimited supply	Often limited (e.g., bitcoin's cap)
Transaction speed	Slow (1-5 days for international)	Fast (minutes or less)
Accessibility	Bank account required	Internet access required
Transparency	Private, but controlled	Public (blockchain ledger)

Example to illustrate the comparison:

Imagine two friends—Sarah in the united states and Juan in argentina. Sarah wants to send $100 to juan. If she uses traditional banking, the money takes three days, incurs a $30 wire fee, and juan loses 10% of the value when converting dollars to pesos due to bad exchange rates.

Now, Sarah tries cryptocurrency. She sends $100 worth of bitcoin. The transaction is complete in minutes, fees are a fraction of the cost, and juan receives the full value without needing a bank account.

While cryptocurrency isn't perfect, its potential to solve real-world problems like this is why it's gaining traction.

By the end of this chapter, you'll have a clear understanding of what cryptocurrency is, why it matters, and how it compares to traditional money. This foundation will prepare you to dive deeper into the exciting world of digital assets in the chapters ahead.

CHAPTER 2: BLOCKCHAIN TECHNOLOGY MADE SIMPLE

The Backbone of Crypto

Blockchain is the technological foundation of cryptocurrency, often referred to as a "digital ledger" or a "record-keeping system." While these terms sound technical, understanding blockchain doesn't have to be overwhelming. Imagine it as a revolutionary way to store and share information securely, transparently, and without needing a middleman.

How Blockchain Works: A Beginner-Friendly Analogy

Let's say you and your friends decide to keep a group expense tracker. Instead of one person managing the tracker (and risking them accidentally—or intentionally—changing numbers), you all agree on a new system:

1. Every time someone spends money, they announce the transaction to the group.

2. Everyone writes it down in their own notebook.

3. At the end of the day, you all compare notes to ensure everyone has the same record. Once confirmed, no one can alter those entries.

This is the essence of blockchain: a decentralized, tamper-proof record where everyone involved holds a copy of the same information. Now, let's add some digital enhancements:

- Instead of human participants, the process is handled by computers.

- Transactions are verified through cryptographic puzzles (a process called "mining" or "validation").

- Once verified, transactions are grouped into "blocks." Each block is linked to the one before it, creating a **chain of blocks**—hence the name blockchain.

Key Features of Blockchain

- **Decentralization:** Unlike traditional systems where a bank or company manages data, blockchain operates on a network of computers (called nodes). No single entity has control.

- **Immutability:** Once a block is added to the chain, it cannot be altered. This makes blockchain tamper-proof.

- **Transparency:** Every participant in the network can see the transactions on the blockchain, ensuring accountability.

The Concept of Decentralization and Distributed Ledgers

Traditional systems—like banks—rely on centralization. A single institution holds all the power, records, and decision-making authority. For example:

- When you send money via your bank, the bank verifies and approves the transaction.

- If their system crashes or is hacked, your data could be at risk.

Blockchain flips this model upside down through **decentralization**:

- Instead of one central authority, many computers in the network share responsibility for maintaining the ledger.

- This ledger—known as a **distributed ledger**—is stored on every participating computer. If one computer goes offline, the others keep the system running.

Real-World Examples

Bitcoin's Blockchain

Bitcoin, the first cryptocurrency, operates on a simple blockchain designed to record transactions. Here's how it works:

- Alice wants to send 1 Bitcoin to Bob.

- The transaction is broadcast to the Bitcoin network, where computers (miners) verify it.

- Once verified, the transaction is added to a new block.

- That block is linked to previous blocks, forming an unbroken chain.

Bitcoin's blockchain is **single-purpose**—it only handles transactions. Think of it as a secure, global checkbook.

Ethereum's Blockchain

Ethereum's blockchain takes things a step further. While it also processes transactions, it introduces **smart contracts**—self-executing agreements with terms written into code.

- Example: Imagine renting an apartment using Ethereum. The smart contract might state, "If Bob pays 1 Ether, release the digital key to the apartment." The contract executes automatically when conditions are met, removing the need for intermediaries like landlords or agents.

Ethereum's flexibility has made it the backbone for decentralized apps (dapps), non-fungible tokens (nfts), and decentralized finance (defi).

Key Difference:

- **Bitcoin's blockchain** is like a calculator: reliable for one task.

- **Ethereum's blockchain** is like a smartphone: versatile and programmable.

Applications Beyond Crypto

Blockchain isn't just for cryptocurrency. Its unique features—security, transparency, and decentralization—make it valuable in countless industries.

Supply Chain Management

One of blockchain's most promising applications is in tracking goods as they move through the supply chain.

- **Example:** Imagine buying a chocolate bar labeled "ethically sourced." How can you be sure the cocoa was farmed responsibly? With blockchain, each step of the supply chain—from farm to store—is recorded on an immutable ledger. You can scan a code on the chocolate bar and instantly access its entire journey.

- Companies like Walmart are already using blockchain to trace food origins, reducing fraud and improving food safety.

Healthcare

In healthcare, blockchain can revolutionize how patient data is stored and shared:

- **Example:** Currently, your medical records are scattered across hospitals, clinics, and labs. If you switch doctors, transferring your records can be a hassle. With blockchain, your records could be stored securely and accessed instantly by authorized personnel, no matter where you go.

- This reduces errors, ensures privacy, and empowers patients to control their own data.

Digital Identity

Blockchain offers a solution to identity theft and data breaches by giving individuals control over their own identities.

- **Example:** Instead of providing a company with all your personal details (name, address, ID number), you could share only the necessary information via a secure blockchain. Companies like Microsoft are exploring blockchain-based identity solutions.

Voting Systems

Imagine casting your vote in an election from the comfort of your home, knowing it's tamper-proof. Blockchain's transparency and immutability make it ideal for secure, verifiable voting.

- **Example:** In 2020, blockchain-based voting was piloted in Utah for overseas voters, showing early signs of success.

The Power of Blockchain

Blockchain is more than just the backbone of cryptocurrency; it's a transformative technology with the potential to disrupt industries, improve efficiency, and empower individuals. As we delve deeper into cryptocurrency, understanding blockchain is crucial. It's not just a buzzword—it's the engine driving the digital revolution.

By the end of this chapter, you'll see blockchain not as a complex, intimidating concept but as a tool with endless possibilities, shaping the future of finance, commerce, and beyond.

CHAPTER 3: TYPES OF CRYPTOCURRENCIES

Not all cryptocurrencies are created equal. While many people think of cryptocurrency as a single concept—like bitcoin—the truth is the crypto space is incredibly diverse, with different types of coins serving different purposes. This chapter breaks down the key categories, provides examples of popular cryptocurrencies, and introduces you to the fascinating world of altcoins.

The categories of coins

1. Payment coins

These are the original cryptocurrencies, designed primarily as a medium of exchange or "digital cash." bitcoin is the most famous example, but many other coins also aim to facilitate fast, secure, and cost-effective transactions.

Examples:

- **Bitcoin (btc):** often referred to as "digital gold," bitcoin was created to be a decentralized alternative to traditional money. Its fixed supply of 21 million coins ensures scarcity, which has helped it retain value over time.

    - *Use case:* buying goods and services, cross-border payments, or storing value as an investment.

- **Litecoin (ltc):** known as "the silver to bitcoin's gold," litecoin is faster and cheaper for everyday transactions, making it a practical payment coin.

Why payment coins matter:

they offer a way to transfer value globally without relying on banks or intermediaries, reducing costs and increasing financial access.

2. Stablecoins

Stablecoins are designed to solve one of cryptocurrency's biggest challenges: **volatility**. Their value is pegged to a stable asset like the us dollar, gold, or even a basket of currencies. This stability makes them ideal for transactions and as a "safe haven" during market downturns.

Examples:

- **Usdt (tether):** pegged to the us dollar, usdt is widely used for trading and transferring funds without worrying about price fluctuations.

- **Usdc (usd coin):** another dollar-pegged stablecoin, known for its transparency and full backing by reserves.

Use case:

- If you're trading cryptocurrencies and want to "cash out" without leaving the market, you can convert your holdings to a stablecoin like usdc or usdt. This lets you avoid volatility while keeping your funds in the crypto ecosystem.

3. Utility tokens

Utility tokens provide access to specific services or products within a blockchain ecosystem. Unlike payment coins, these tokens have a more specialized role.

Examples:

- **Bnb (binance coin):** originally created to reduce trading fees on the binance exchange, bnb has evolved into a versatile token used for payments, transaction fees, and more.

- **Filecoin (fil):** this token is used within the filecoin network to buy decentralized storage space, offering an alternative to traditional cloud storage providers like google drive

Why utility tokens matter:

they power decentralized platforms and create real-world value by enabling services that traditional systems can't easily replicate.

4. Nfts (non-fungible tokens)

Nfts represent unique digital assets that cannot be exchanged on a one-to-one basis, unlike bitcoin or dollars. They're primarily used for ownership of digital art, music, virtual real estate, and collectibles.

Examples:

- **Cryptopunks:** early digital art collectibles that became status symbols in the nft world.

- **Bored ape yacht club:** a collection of unique, cartoon-style apes that grant their owners perks like exclusive access to events and communities.

Use case:

- Artists can mint and sell their work as nfts, cutting out traditional middlemen. Buyers, in turn, gain verifiable ownership of a unique digital piece.

Why nfts are revolutionary:

they bring scarcity and ownership to the digital world, creating new ways for creators and consumers to interact.

Profiles of popular cryptocurrencies

Bitcoin: the pioneer

Bitcoin, created in 2009 by the mysterious satoshi nakamoto, was the first cryptocurrency and remains the most valuable. Its main purpose is to act as "digital gold"—a store of value and a hedge against inflation.

Why bitcoin stands out:

- **Scarcity:** with only 21 million coins ever to exist, bitcoin's value is driven by limited supply.

- **Security:** bitcoin's blockchain is the most secure, with thousands of nodes maintaining and validating the network.

- **Adoption:** it's the most widely recognized cryptocurrency, accepted by major companies like tesla (briefly), microsoft, and paypal.

Example:

el salvador made headlines by adopting bitcoin as legal tender, enabling citizens to use it for everyday purchases and cross-border remittances.

Ethereum: the smart contract king

Ethereum is more than just a cryptocurrency—it's a programmable blockchain that allows developers to create decentralized applications (dapps) and smart contracts. Launched in 2015 by vitalik buterin, ethereum introduced flexibility to blockchain technology.

Key features:

- **Smart contracts:** self-executing agreements with terms written directly into code. For instance, an insurance payout could be triggered automatically based on weather data.

- **Ecosystem:** ethereum powers defi (decentralized finance), nfts, and dapps, making it the backbone of many blockchain innovations.

Example:

nft marketplaces like opensea and defi platforms like uniswap operate on ethereum's blockchain.

Stablecoins: the promise of stability

While bitcoin and ethereum dominate headlines, stablecoins play a critical role in the crypto ecosystem. By offering stability, they bridge the gap between traditional finance and the volatile crypto market.

Popular stablecoins:

- **Usdt (tether):** the most traded stablecoin, widely used for transferring value and trading pairs.

- **Usdc (usd coin):** known for its transparency, each usdc is backed by a dollar held in reserve.

Example:

imagine you're a freelancer working for international clients. By getting paid in usdc, you avoid slow bank transfers, high fees, and currency conversion hassles.

The world of altcoins

Altcoins, or "alternative coins," refer to any cryptocurrency that isn't bitcoin. They range from serious projects with unique use cases to playful experiments that have captured public attention.

Solana: the speed demon

Solana is known for its lightning-fast transaction speeds and low fees. It's often called an "ethereum killer" due to its ability to handle thousands of transactions per second.

Use case:

- Solana is a popular choice for gaming platforms and nft projects because of its efficiency and cost-effectiveness.

Cardano: the academic blockchain

Founded by charles hoskinson, one of ethereum's co-creators, cardano prides itself on being a scientifically driven blockchain. It focuses on sustainability, scalability, and security.

Use case:

- Cardano is working on projects like digital identity solutions for underbanked populations in africa.

Dogecoin: the meme coin

Originally created as a joke, dogecoin gained popularity thanks to its fun-loving community and celebrity endorsements from figures like elon musk.

Why it's unique:

- Dogecoin has no hard cap on supply, which means it's not inherently scarce. However, its charm lies in its community-driven ethos.

Example:

in 2021, dogecoin saw a massive price surge as it became a symbol of internet culture and grassroots enthusiasm.

The bigger picture

Cryptocurrency has evolved far beyond bitcoin, with different types of coins addressing different needs and industries. From payment coins and stablecoins to nfts and altcoins, the crypto landscape offers something for everyone. Understanding these categories will help you identify opportunities that align with your financial goals and interests as we dive deeper into the world of cryptocurrency in the next chapters.

CHAPTER 4: HOW TO BUY AND STORE CRYPTOCURRENCY

For many newcomers, buying cryptocurrency can feel like stepping into uncharted territory. The good news? It's simpler than you think, especially when you break it down into manageable steps. This chapter will walk you through the process of buying your first cryptocurrency, setting up an account on an exchange, and ensuring your assets are stored securely.

Getting started

The first step in entering the cryptocurrency market is choosing a platform to buy and trade your digital assets. These platforms, called cryptocurrency exchanges, act as digital marketplaces where buyers and sellers come together to trade.

Choosing an exchange

There are countless exchanges out there, each with its own strengths, weaknesses, and user experience. When choosing an exchange, consider the following factors:

1. **Security:**

    your funds and personal data need to be safe. Look for exchanges with strong security measures, such as two-factor authentication (2fa) and insurance for stored assets.

    - *Example:* coinbase is known for its user-friendly interface and high security standards, making it a great option for beginners.

2. **Fees:**

    most exchanges charge fees for trading, depositing, and withdrawing. These fees can vary significantly, so it's worth comparing platforms to find the best deal for your needs.

    - *Example:* binance offers some of the lowest fees in the industry, especially if you use its native token, bnb, to pay for transactions.

3. **Supported cryptocurrencies:**

some exchanges only offer a limited number of coins. Make sure the platform you choose supports the cryptocurrencies you're interested in buying.

- *Example:* kraken is known for supporting a wide variety of cryptocurrencies, from popular options like bitcoin and ethereum to lesser-known altcoins.

4. **User experience:**

as a beginner, ease of use is critical. Platforms like coinbase and kraken prioritize intuitive design, while advanced traders might prefer exchanges like binance or kucoin for their range of tools and options.

Pro tip: always check user reviews and do some research before committing to an exchange. Scams and poorly managed platforms can cost you money and time.

Setting up your account

Once you've chosen an exchange, setting up your account is the next step. Most reputable exchanges follow strict regulations to ensure safety and compliance, which means you'll need to verify your identity before you can trade.

1. **Registering your account:**

- Provide a valid email address and create a strong password.

- Set up two-factor authentication (2fa) to add an extra layer of security. This usually involves linking your account to an app like google authenticator or receiving verification codes via sms.

2. **Completing kyc (know your customer):**

    to comply with regulations, most exchanges require you to submit identification documents. This process, known as kyc, is designed to prevent fraud and money laundering.

- You'll typically need to upload a government-issued id (like a passport or driver's license) and proof of address (such as a utility bill).

- While it may seem like a hassle, completing kyc ensures your account is secure and compliant.

3. Depositing funds:

- Many exchanges let you deposit fiat currency (like usd, eur, or php) via bank transfer, credit card, or even paypal.

- Alternatively, if you already own cryptocurrency, you can deposit it directly into your exchange wallet.

-
4. Buying cryptocurrency:
- Once your account is funded, you're ready to buy! Search for the cryptocurrency you want (e.g., bitcoin or ethereum), specify the amount, and confirm the transaction. Most platforms will show you the equivalent value in fiat currency for transparency.

Example:
let's say you deposit $100 into your coinbase

account. You decide to buy bitcoin and confirm the transaction. Within minutes, your account reflects your newly acquired bitcoin. Congratulations—you're now a cryptocurrency owner!

Securing your assets

Buying cryptocurrency is only half the battle. The next crucial step is to store your assets securely. Unlike traditional money stored in a bank, cryptocurrency requires a more hands-on approach to safeguarding.

Hot wallets vs. Cold wallets

What is a wallet?

A cryptocurrency wallet is a digital tool that stores your private keys—the credentials that allow you to access and manage your crypto assets. Without these keys, you can't access your funds.

1. **Hot wallets:**

    these are wallets connected to the internet, making them convenient but more vulnerable to hacks. Hot wallets are best for frequent trading or small amounts of cryptocurrency.

- **Examples of hot wallets:**

    o **Exchange wallets:** wallets provided by your chosen exchange (e.g., binance or coinbase). While convenient, keeping large amounts of cryptocurrency on an exchange is risky due to potential hacks.

    o **Mobile/online wallets:** apps like trust wallet and metamask allow you to store crypto on your phone or browser.

Use case:

if you're actively trading or making daily transactions, a hot wallet provides quick access.

2. Cold wallets:

cold wallets are offline wallets that aren't connected to the internet, making them much more secure. They're ideal for storing large amounts of cryptocurrency for the long term.

- **Examples of cold wallets:**
    - **Hardware wallets:** devices like ledger nano x or trezor. These small usb-like devices store your private keys offline.

    - **Paper wallets:** a physical piece of paper with your private keys and wallet address printed on it. While secure, losing the paper means losing access to your crypto.

Use case:

if you've purchased cryptocurrency as a long-term investment, consider transferring it to a hardware wallet for maximum security.

Understanding private keys and seed phrases

Your private keys and seed phrases are the most important elements of cryptocurrency security. Think of them as the keys to your digital safe.

1. **Private keys:**

    Aprivate key is a unique string of characters that grants you access to your cryptocurrency. Losing this key means losing your funds, as no central authority can recover it for you.

2. Seed phrases:

When setting up a wallet, you'll often be given a **seed phrase**—a list of 12–24 random words that serve as a backup for your private keys.

- *Example:* if your hardware wallet is lost or damaged, you can restore access to your funds by entering the seed phrase into a new device.

Pro tips for securing keys and phrases:

- Write your seed phrase down on paper and store it in a safe place (avoid saving it digitally, as hackers could access it).

- Consider storing copies in multiple secure locations, like a fireproof safe or safety deposit box.

Final thoughts

Buying and storing cryptocurrency doesn't have to be intimidating. By choosing a reputable exchange, completing a secure setup, and using the right wallet for your needs, you can confidently enter the world of crypto. Remember, cryptocurrency puts the power of financial freedom in your hands—but with great power comes great responsibility. Taking the time to secure your assets ensures you're prepared for the exciting journey ahead.

CHAPTER 5: RISK AND REWARD

Investing in cryptocurrency can be exhilarating, but it's not without its challenges. This chapter dives deep into the unique risks and rewards of the crypto market, equipping you with the knowledge to navigate volatility, avoid common pitfalls, and learn from real-world examples of triumphs and tragedies.

Volatility and market risks

Cryptocurrency is infamous for its volatility. While dramatic price swings can lead to massive gains, they can just as easily wipe out your investment overnight. To understand why crypto prices fluctuate so dramatically, we need to explore some key factors driving this market behavior.

Why crypto prices fluctuate dramatically

1. **Limited market maturity:**

   Cryptocurrency is still a relatively young market compared to traditional assets like stocks and bonds. With lower trading volumes and less liquidity, even a small influx or outflow of capital can cause significant price swings.

Example:

when tesla announced it had purchased $1.5 billion in bitcoin in 2021, bitcoin's price surged nearly 20% in a single day. Conversely, when elon musk tweeted concerns about bitcoin's environmental impact, its price dropped by over 10%.

2. **Speculation and hype:**

   much of the cryptocurrency market is driven by speculation. Traders often buy based on future potential rather than current utility, leading to inflated prices that can crash if expectations aren't met.

Example:

shiba inu, a meme coin, saw a meteoric rise of over 1,000% in october 2021, fueled purely by social media hype. A few weeks later, it lost much of its value, leaving late investors with heavy losses.

3. **Lack of regulation:**

   Unlike traditional financial markets, cryptocurrency operates in a largely unregulated environment. This creates opportunities for manipulation, such as "pump and dump" schemes where groups artificially inflate prices and sell at a profit, leaving others to bear the losses.

The role of market sentiment and news

In the crypto world, sentiment and news can move markets faster and more dramatically than in traditional finance.

1. **Media influence:**

   positive news, like a major company accepting bitcoin or a country adopting cryptocurrency, can trigger massive buying sprees. Conversely, regulatory crackdowns or negative press can spark widespread panic selling.

- *Example:* when China banned cryptocurrency mining in 2021, bitcoin's price dropped by 50% within weeks.

2. **Social media and influencers:**

Tweets, youtube videos, and reddit forums wield immense power in shaping market sentiment. A single post by a popular influencer can send a coin's price soaring—or crashing.

- *Example:* Elon Musk's infamous tweets about dogecoin caused its price to spike by over 300% in early 2021, only for it to tumble when interest waned.

3. **Fear and greed:**

the crypto market is heavily influenced by human emotions. When prices rise, greed drives investors to pile in, fearing they'll miss out on gains. When prices fall, fear takes over, leading to panic selling.

Common pitfalls for new investors

While the potential for reward in crypto is high, so too are the risks—especially for those who are new to the space. Being aware of common pitfalls can save you from costly mistakes.

Scams: rug pulls, phishing, and ponzi schemes

Cryptocurrency is a haven for innovation, but it's also a playground for scammers. Knowing the common schemes can help you avoid becoming a victim.

1. **Rug pulls:**

    in a rug pull, developers launch a new cryptocurrency project, hype it up to attract investors, and then vanish with the funds.
    - *Example:* in 2021, the creators of a cryptocurrency called squid game token (unaffiliated with the netflix show) pulled a rug pull, stealing millions of dollars from investors before disappearing.

2. **Phishing attacks:**

   Hackers often create fake websites or send fraudulent emails to trick investors into revealing their private keys or seed phrases.

   - *Example:* you receive an email claiming to be from your exchange, asking you to "verify your account" by entering your wallet details. Once you do, your funds are stolen.

3. **Ponzi schemes:**

   these scams promise high returns for early investors, funded by money from newer participants. When new investments dry up, the scheme collapses.

   - *Example:* bitconnect, a notorious ponzi scheme, promised investors up to 1% daily returns. It collapsed in 2018, wiping out billions of dollars.

Emotional trading and the fear of missing out (fomo)

Many new investors fall victim to their emotions, making impulsive decisions that lead to losses.

1. **The danger of fomo:**

   when prices are skyrocketing, it's tempting to jump in, fearing you'll miss out on gains. But buying at the peak often leads to heavy losses when prices correct.

   - *Example:* during bitcoin's bull run in late 2017, many investors bought in at $19,000, only to see its price crash to $3,000 in 2018.

2. **Panic selling:**

   when the market dips, fear takes over, leading investors to sell at a loss rather than riding out the volatility.

   - *Example:* if you bought ethereum at $4,000 in 2021 and sold during a dip at $2,000 out of fear, you would have missed its eventual recovery.
   -

Pro tip:

set clear investment goals and stick to them. Avoid making decisions based on emotion. Dollar-cost averaging—investing a fixed amount at regular intervals—can help mitigate the impact of volatility.

Case studies

Learning from real-world examples can provide valuable insights into the highs and lows of the crypto market.

Massive gains: the rise of bitcoin millionaires

Bitcoin's rise from obscurity to mainstream recognition has created countless millionaires.

- *Example:* Erik Finman invested $1,000 in bitcoin at age 12 when it was priced at just $12 per coin. By 2021, his holdings were worth millions.

- **Lesson:** early adoption and patience can yield extraordinary rewards, but this kind of success is rare and requires a high tolerance for risk.

Devastating losses: the bitconnect collapse

Bitconnect lured investors with promises of guaranteed high returns through its lending platform. At its peak, the project had a market cap of over $2 billion. When it collapsed in 2018, investors lost everything.

- **Lesson:** if something sounds too good to be true, it probably is. Always research a project thoroughly before investing.

The story of luna and terrausd

In 2022, terrausd (a stablecoin) and its companion cryptocurrency, luna, were part of a groundbreaking algorithmic ecosystem. When the system failed, both coins lost nearly all their value within days, wiping out billions in investor funds.

- **Lesson:** even "stable" investments can carry significant risk. Diversify your portfolio to avoid overexposure to a single asset.

Final thoughts

The cryptocurrency market is a double-edged sword: its volatility creates opportunities for life-changing gains but also poses significant risks. By understanding the factors driving market behavior, avoiding common pitfalls, and learning from the experiences of others, you can navigate this dynamic space with confidence. Remember, the key to success is preparation, discipline, and a willingness to learn.

CHAPTER 6: BUILDING A CRYPTO PORTFOLIO

Building a strong cryptocurrency portfolio is much like constructing a sturdy house: you need a solid foundation, carefully chosen materials, and a clear blueprint. In this chapter, we'll explore how to allocate your investments, balance risk, and set realistic goals to create a portfolio that suits your needs and risk tolerance.

Allocating your investments

A well-constructed crypto portfolio balances potential rewards with manageable risks. To achieve this, you'll need to carefully consider how you allocate your funds across different types of cryptocurrencies.

Balancing risk with blue-chip cryptocurrencies vs. Altcoins

1. **Blue-chip cryptocurrencies:**

   these are the established giants of the crypto world, such as bitcoin (btc) and ethereum (eth). They're considered less risky because of their proven track records, high adoption rates, and robust infrastructure.

   - *Example:* bitcoin, often called "digital gold," has demonstrated relative stability compared to smaller cryptocurrencies. While it's still volatile, it has weathered market cycles and continues to be a reliable store of value.

   - *Portfolio allocation:* for beginners or conservative investors, dedicating 50–70% of your portfolio to blue-chip cryptocurrencies is a safe starting point.

2. **Altcoins:**

   altcoins include all cryptocurrencies outside of bitcoin and ethereum. These range from established coins like cardano (ada) and solana (sol) to riskier, lesser-known tokens.

- *Example:* solana offers faster transaction speeds and lower fees than ethereum, making it a popular choice for nfts and defi projects. However, its newer status means it carries higher risks.

- *Portfolio allocation:* allocate 20–40% of your portfolio to carefully researched altcoins. These investments have higher growth potential but come with greater risk

3. **Meme coins and high-risk tokens:**

meme coins like dogecoin and shiba inu are highly speculative and driven by hype rather than utility. While they can generate massive short-term gains, they're also prone to sudden crashes.

- *Example:* dogecoin surged by over 300% in 2021, fueled by Elon Musk's tweets, but it later lost much of its value.

- *Portfolio allocation:* limit high-risk tokens to 5–10% of your portfolio, if at all.

Pro tip: treat cryptocurrency allocation like seasoning a dish: focus on the essentials (blue-chip cryptocurrencies), then add smaller portions of riskier assets for flavor.

Diversifying across blockchain sectors

Cryptocurrencies serve different purposes within the blockchain ecosystem. Diversifying across sectors can help you spread risk and capture opportunities in multiple areas of innovation.

1. **Smart contract platforms:**

   these are the "operating systems" of blockchain, enabling decentralized applications (dapps).

   - *Examples:* ethereum (eth), cardano (ada), solana (sol).

   - *Why it matters:* these platforms are foundational to defi, nfts, and other blockchain innovations.

2. **Decentralized finance (defi):** defi coins power financial services like lending, borrowing, and trading without banks.

    - *Examples:* aave (aave), uniswap (uni), compound (comp).

    - *Why it matters:* defi is disrupting traditional banking, with significant growth potential.

3. **Gaming and metaverse tokens:**

   these tokens fuel blockchain-based games and virtual worlds.

    - *Examples:* axie infinity (axs), decentraland (mana), the sandbox (sand).

    - *Why it matters:* the gaming and metaverse sectors are rapidly expanding, attracting mainstream attention.

4. **Stablecoins:**

    while not typically growth assets, stablecoins like usdt and usdc can act as a hedge during market downturns.

    - *Why it matters:* keeping 5–10% of your portfolio in stablecoins provides liquidity for future investments.

Setting investment goals

Before investing in cryptocurrency, it's essential to clarify your financial goals and align your strategy accordingly. Are you aiming for quick profits, long-term wealth accumulation, or a mix of both?

Short-term trading vs. Long-term holding (hodling)

1. **Short-term trading:**

    short-term traders aim to profit from market volatility by buying low and selling high within days or weeks. This approach requires active monitoring and a solid understanding of technical analysis.
    - *Example:* a trader might buy

ethereum during a dip at $1,500 and sell it a week later at $1,700, pocketing the difference.

- **Pros:** potential for quick gains.

- **Cons:** high risk, time-intensive, and emotionally taxing.

2. **Long-term holding (hodling):**

   hodling involves buying cryptocurrencies and holding them for years, regardless of short-term price fluctuations. This strategy is based on the belief that the value of quality assets will increase over time.

   - *Example:* if you had purchased bitcoin in 2013 for $100 and held it until 2023, your investment would have grown exponentially.

   - **Pros:** less stress, no need for daily monitoring, and ideal for beginners.

   - **Cons:** requires patience and the ability to weather market downturns.

Pro tip: combine both strategies by allocating a portion of your portfolio for long-term holding while using a smaller percentage for short-term trades.

Dollar-cost averaging: mitigating risk

Dollar-cost averaging (dca) is a simple yet effective strategy for reducing the impact of market volatility. Instead of investing a lump sum all at once, you invest a fixed amount at regular intervals, such as weekly or monthly.

How it works:

- Let's say you want to invest $1,000 in bitcoin. Rather than buying $1,000 worth today, you invest $100 every week for 10 weeks. This approach spreads out your purchases, allowing you to buy more bitcoin when prices are low and less WHEN PRICES ARE HIGH.

Benefits of dca:

1. **Reduces emotional decision-making:**

    you're less likely to panic during market dips or get greedy during spikes.

2. **Mitigates volatility:** by averaging your entry price, you avoid the risk of buying all your crypto at a market peak.

3. **Fits any budget:** you don't need a large initial investment—dca works with as little as $10 per interval.

Example:

if you started dca into ethereum in january 2020 by investing $100 monthly, you would have benefited from lower prices early on and significant gains as ethereum's value skyrocketed in subsequent years.

Building your personalized crypto portfolio

Here's a sample allocation for a beginner investor with $1,000 to invest:

- **50% ($500): blue-chip cryptocurrencies**

    o $300 in bitcoin (btc).
    o $200 in ethereum (eth).

- **30% ($300): altcoins across different sectors**

    - $100 in solana (sol) (smart contracts).
    - $100 in aave (aave) (defi).
    - $100 in axie infinity (axs) (gaming).

- **10% ($100): high-risk meme coins or experimental projects**

    - $100 in dogecoin (doge).

- **10% ($100): stablecoins for liquidity**

    - $100 in usdc or usdt.

Final thoughts

Building a crypto portfolio is both an art and a science. By carefully allocating your investments, diversifying across sectors, and setting clear goals, you can create a portfolio that aligns with your risk tolerance and financial aspirations. Remember, the key to success is discipline, patience, and a commitment to continuous learning. As the crypto market evolves, so too should your strategy—always be ready to adapt and grow.

CHAPTER 7: THE ART OF TIMING

Timing is everything in cryptocurrency. Unlike traditional markets, which often move predictably due to established rules and large institutional players, crypto operates in a highly volatile, 24/7 global environment. Understanding market cycles and mastering basic technical analysis can significantly enhance your ability to make informed decisions about when to buy, sell, or hold. In this chapter, we'll explore the dynamics of market cycles, historical trends, and the tools traders use to read charts effectively.

Market Cycles in Crypto

Cryptocurrency markets are cyclical, swinging between periods of rapid growth (bull runs) and prolonged declines (bear markets). Recognizing these patterns can help you capitalize on opportunities while avoiding common pitfalls.

Bull Runs and Bear Markets

1. **Bull Runs:**

   A bull run refers to a sustained period of rising prices, often fueled by increasing demand, hype, and positive sentiment. During these periods, new investors flood the market, pushing prices higher.

   - *Example:* The 2017 bull run saw Bitcoin rise from $1,000 in January to nearly $20,000 by December, driven by mainstream media coverage and widespread FOMO (fear of missing out).

2. **Bear Markets:**

   A bear market, on the other hand, is characterized by falling prices, negative sentiment, and reduced trading activity. Bear markets can last months or even years, testing the patience and resolve of investors.

   - *Example:* After the 2017 bull run, Bitcoin entered a bear market in 2018, dropping to as low as $3,000 by the end of the year. Many who bought at the peak sold at a loss, fearing further declines.

The Impact of Bitcoin Halvings

Bitcoin halvings are key events that significantly influence market cycles. A halving occurs approximately every four years, reducing the reward miners receive for validating transactions by 50%. This reduction in supply, combined with steady or increasing demand, often leads to price surges.

How Halvings Work:

- Bitcoin's total supply is capped at 21 million coins. To control its issuance rate, the reward for mining new blocks is halved every 210,000 blocks (roughly four years).

Historical Impact of Halvings:

- **2012 Halving:** Bitcoin's price rose from $12 to over $1,100 within a year of the event.

- **2016 Halving:** Bitcoin increased from $650 to $20,000 during the subsequent bull run in 2017.

- **2020 Halving:** Bitcoin surged from $8,000 to an all-time high of $69,000 in 2021, driven by institutional adoption and mainstream interest.

Key Insight:

While halvings don't immediately trigger price spikes, they create a supply shock that often sets the stage for bull runs in the months that follow.

Historical Analysis of Price Trends

Studying historical trends can provide valuable insights into market behavior. Although past performance doesn't guarantee future results, patterns often repeat due to human psychology and market dynamics.

Bitcoin's Four-Year Cycle:

1. **Year of the Halving:** Prices begin to rise as supply reduces.

2. **Post-Halving Bull Run:** Massive growth follows as demand outweighs supply.

3. **Market Correction:** Prices stabilize or drop as the market cools down.

4. **Accumulation Phase:** Investors and institutions quietly accumulate during low prices, preparing for the next cycle.

Example:

During the 2018 bear market, savvy investors accumulated Bitcoin at low prices. When the 2020 halving occurred, they reaped significant rewards during the subsequent bull run.

Reading the Charts

While market cycles give you the bigger picture, technical analysis (TA) provides tools to make short- and medium-term decisions. By learning to interpret price charts, you can identify patterns and trends, helping you determine when to buy, sell, or hold.

Basics of Technical Analysis: Support, Resistance, and Trends

1. **Support and Resistance Levels:**

    o **Support:** A price level where an asset tends to stop falling and bounce back up due to increased buying interest.

- **Resistance:** A price level where an asset tends to stop rising and pull back due to increased selling pressure.

Example:

If Bitcoin consistently bounces back at $20,000, that level is considered support. If it struggles to break past $25,000, that's a resistance level.

Why It Matters:

Recognizing these levels helps you time your entry and exit points. Buying near support and selling near resistance is a common strategy.

2. **Trends:**

    - **Uptrend:** A series of higher highs and higher lows, indicating a bullish market.

    - **Downtrend:** A series of lower highs and lower lows, signaling a bearish market.

    - **Sideways Trend:** When prices move within a range, neither rising nor falling significantly.

Why It Matters:

Understanding the current trend helps you align your trades with market momentum, increasing the likelihood of success.

Tools for Technical Analysis

Several tools and indicators can help you analyze price movements and predict potential trends. While there are many advanced techniques, here are three beginner-friendly tools:

1. **Relative Strength Index (RSI):** The RSI measures the speed and magnitude of price changes, indicating whether an asset is overbought or oversold.

    - **Overbought (above 70):** A signal that the asset may be due for a price correction.

    - **Oversold (below 30):** A signal that the asset might be undervalued and ready for a bounce.

    - *Example:* If Ethereum's RSI is 80, it might be a good time to sell and

lock in profits before a pullback.
2. **Moving Averages (MA):**

Moving averages smooth out price data, helping you identify trends over time.

- **Simple Moving Average (SMA):** Calculates the average price over a specific period (e.g., 50 days).

- **Exponential Moving Average (EMA):** Gives more weight to recent prices, making it more responsive to current trends.

- *Example:* If Bitcoin's price is above its 200-day SMA, it's generally considered bullish.

3. **MACD (Moving Average Convergence Divergence):**

The MACD is a momentum indicator that shows the relationship between two moving averages. It's used to identify trend reversals and momentum shifts.

- **Bullish Signal:** When the MACD line crosses above the signal line.

- **Bearish Signal:** When the MACD line crosses below the signal line.

- *Example:* If the MACD crosses upward while Bitcoin is approaching a support level, it could be a strong buy signal.

Putting It All Together

Let's combine what we've learned in a practical scenario:

1. **You identify a support level for Ethereum at $1,500.**

2. **The RSI indicates oversold conditions (below 30), suggesting a potential bounce.**

3. **The MACD shows a bullish crossover, confirming upward momentum.**

Based on this analysis, you decide to buy Ethereum at $1,500. Over the next week, the price rises to $1,800, and you sell for a 20% profit.

Final Thoughts

Mastering the art of timing in cryptocurrency requires a combination of understanding market cycles and honing your technical analysis skills. While no strategy guarantees success, being informed and disciplined significantly increases your chances of making profitable decisions. Remember, timing the market perfectly is nearly impossible, but by studying patterns, trends, and historical data, you can position yourself to ride the waves of the crypto market more effectively.

CHAPTER 8: STAKING, LENDING, AND EARNING YIELD

One of the most exciting aspects of cryptocurrency is the ability to generate passive income. Unlike traditional investments, crypto offers unique opportunities to earn rewards without selling your assets. Whether through staking, lending, or yield farming, you can make your money work for you. However, these opportunities come with their own set of risks and challenges. In this chapter, we'll explore how to earn passive income with crypto, dive into the mechanics of staking and lending, and provide tips to avoid pitfalls along the way.

Passive income opportunities

Staking: earning rewards on proof-of-stake networks

Staking is a popular way to earn passive income in the cryptocurrency world, particularly on **proof-of-stake (pos)** networks. Unlike bitcoin's **proof-**

of-work system, which relies on energy-intensive mining, pos networks allow users to "stake" their cryptocurrency to support the network and validate transactions.

How staking works:

1. You lock a certain amount of cryptocurrency in a network wallet (known as staking).

2. The network uses your staked assets to help validate transactions and maintain security.

3. In return, you earn rewards, typically paid in the same cryptocurrency.

Example of staking:

- **Ethereum (eth):** after transitioning to pos, ethereum allows users to stake eth to help secure the network. By staking eth on platforms like lido or directly through ethereum validators, users earn annual rewards, often around 4–8%.

- **Cardano (ada):** by staking ada in a pool, users can earn rewards of approximately 4–5% annually without locking their funds (most cardano pools offer flexibility).

Benefits of staking:

- Steady and predictable rewards.
- Supports the network's security and operations.
- Easier to participate than traditional mining.

Risks of staking:

- **Lock-up periods:** some networks require you to lock your staked funds for a certain period, during which you can't access or trade them.

    o *Example:* ethereum staking requires a lock-up until a specific network upgrade, which could take months or years.

- **Price volatility:** while you earn rewards, the value of your staked crypto may drop significantly during market downturns.

Lending platforms: risks and rewards

Lending platforms allow you to loan your cryptocurrency to other users or institutions in exchange for interest payments. This process is usually facilitated through **defi (decentralized finance)** protocols or **cefi (centralized finance)** platforms.

How crypto lending works:

1. You deposit your cryptocurrency into a lending platform like aave (defi) or celsius (cefi).

2. Borrowers take loans using your crypto as liquidity, paying interest on the borrowed funds.

3. You earn a share of the interest as a reward for providing liquidity.

Examples of lending platforms:

- **Defi lending (decentralized):**
    - Aave and compound allow you to lend assets like usdc or eth directly through smart contracts.

- *Example:* lend $1,000 in usdc on aave at a 5% apy, earning $50 annually.

- **Cefi lending (centralized):**

  - Platforms like blockfi or nexo manage the lending process for you, often offering fixed rates.

Benefits of lending:

- Passive income with minimal effort.
- Flexibility: most platforms allow you to withdraw your funds at any time.
- High interest rates compared to traditional savings accounts.

Risks of lending:

- **Platform risk:** if the platform is hacked or mismanages funds, your crypto could be lost.

  - *Example:* in 2022, celsius froze withdrawals during market turmoil, leaving many users unable to access their funds.

- **Borrower default:** while many platforms require over-collateralized loans, extreme market conditions can still lead to defaults.

- **Smart contract vulnerabilities:** in defi, bugs in smart contracts can lead to losses.

Avoiding pitfalls

Earning passive income with crypto can be highly rewarding, but it's not without risks. Being aware of potential pitfalls and understanding how rewards are calculated will help you make smarter decisions.

Understanding apy (annual percentage yield)

Apy is the annual return you earn on your staked or lent assets, factoring in compound interest. While platforms often advertise attractive apys, it's crucial to understand the details behind these numbers.

Key considerations:

1. **Realistic expectations:**
2.
    - Platforms may promote apys of 20% or more, but such high returns are

often unsustainable.

- *Example:* a new defi project offering 50% apy may entice investors, but these rates often drop sharply as more participants join the network.

3. **Variable vs. Fixed rates:**

    - Some platforms offer fixed apys, while others fluctuate based on demand and liquidity.

    - *Example:* lending on aave might yield 10% apy one week and 5% the next, depending on borrower demand.

4. **Hidden fees:**

    - Platforms may deduct fees from your rewards, reducing your overall return. Always read the fine print.

Avoiding unsustainable schemes

The crypto space is rife with schemes that promise unrealistic returns. These often collapse, leaving investors with significant losses. Here's how to spot and avoid them:

1. **Too-good-to-be-true returns:**

   if a platform promises guaranteed returns of 50% or more, approach with extreme caution. High returns often come with high risks—or outright scams.

   - *Example:* the collapse of terra's anchor protocol in 2022, which offered 20% apy on stablecoins, wiped out billions when the system failed.

2. **Lack of transparency:**

   legitimate platforms are open about how they generate returns. Avoid projects that refuse to explain their processes or rely heavily on buzzwords.

3. **Ponzi-like behavior:**

   some platforms use funds from new investors to pay returns to earlier participants, a classic ponzi scheme model. When new investments dry up, the system collapses.

   - *Example:* bitconnect lured thousands with promises of massive returns, only to shut down in 2018, leaving investors with heavy losses.

4. **Smart contract risks in defi:** always ensure the platform you use has been audited by a reputable third party. Unsecured smart contracts can be exploited by hackers.

    o *Example:* the poly network hack in 2021 resulted in a $600 million theft due to a vulnerability in its smart contracts.

Final thoughts

Staking, lending, and earning yield are powerful tools for generating passive income in the cryptocurrency space. By understanding how these systems work and staying vigilant against risks, you can make your crypto holdings work for you. Remember, the key to success lies in balancing risk and reward, diversifying your income sources, and being cautious with platforms that promise the moon. With the right approach, you can enjoy steady, sustainable returns while supporting the growth of the blockchain ecosystem.

CHAPTER 9: REGULATION AND TAXATION

Cryptocurrency operates in a space that's often described as the "wild west" of finance. The rapid growth and decentralized nature of the industry have left many governments scrambling to establish clear rules. For investors, understanding the global regulatory landscape and your tax obligations is essential to avoid pitfalls and maximize returns. This chapter explores how governments regulate cryptocurrency, the impact of these rules on the market, and practical strategies for managing your tax obligations.

Global regulatory landscape

The regulatory approach to cryptocurrency varies widely across the globe, reflecting differing priorities, attitudes toward innovation, and concerns over risks like fraud and money laundering.

How governments view and regulate cryptocurrencies

1. **Supportive jurisdictions:**

   some countries view cryptocurrency as a driver of innovation and economic growth, adopting favorable regulations to attract businesses and investors.

   - **Examples:**
     - **El salvador:** made bitcoin legal tender in 2021, encouraging citizens and businesses to use it alongside the us dollar.
     - **Singapore:** implements clear licensing frameworks to regulate crypto exchanges while fostering innovation.

Benefits for investors:

   - In supportive jurisdictions, you can access tax breaks, crypto-friendly banking services, and stable regulatory environments.
   -

2. **Cautious regulators:**

    other countries recognize the potential of cryptocurrency but impose strict rules to minimize risks.

    o **Examples:**

       - **United states:** classifies cryptocurrencies as property, subjecting them to capital gains tax. The sec aggressively monitors icos and other crypto-related activities.

       - **European union:** the markets in crypto-assets (mica) regulation aims to create a unified framework for crypto across member states, balancing innovation with consumer protection.

3. **Hostile stances:**

    some nations see cryptocurrencies as a threat to financial stability and impose outright bans or severe restrictions.

- **Examples:**

    - **China:** banned cryptocurrency mining and trading in 2021, citing concerns over capital outflows and energy consumption.

      India: while not banned, the government has imposed heavy taxes on crypto gains and discussed restrictions to curb speculative trading.

The impact of regulations on market prices

Regulations—or even the rumor of them—can significantly influence crypto market prices.

1. **Positive impact:**

    clear and supportive regulations often boost investor confidence, attracting institutional money and driving up prices.

    - *Example:* when the european union announced mica in 2022, it provided clarity on crypto rules, encouraging investments across the region.

2. **Negative impact:**

   unfavorable or uncertain regulations can trigger sell-offs, reducing market value.
   - *Example:* china's 2021 ban on cryptocurrency mining caused bitcoin's price to drop by 30% within weeks.

Pro tip: stay informed about regulatory developments in major markets like the us, eu, and asia. These regions often set the tone for global trends.

Tax obligations

Cryptocurrency taxation is one of the most misunderstood aspects of investing in this space. While rules vary by country, most governments treat crypto as property or a financial asset, making gains taxable events.

Reporting crypto gains and losses

1. **What is taxable?**

   - **Capital gains:** if you sell, trade, or use cryptocurrency and its value has increased since you acquired it, you owe taxes on the gain.

- *Example:* if you buy 1 bitcoin for $20,000 and sell it for $30,000, you have a $10,000 capital gain

  o **Income tax:** rewards from staking, mining, or airdrops are often classified as income and taxed accordingly.

  - *Example:* if you earn $1,000 worth of eth from staking, that $1,000 is considered taxable income.

2. **How to track transactions:** keeping accurate records is essential for calculating taxes. Many investors use crypto tax software like **cointracker** or **koinly** to track trades, calculate gains, and generate reports.

   o *What to record:*
   - Dates of acquisition and disposal.
   - Amounts involved.
   - Cost basis (the original price paid).

3. **Reporting losses:**

   losses can offset gains, reducing your taxable amount.

   o *Example:* if you make a $5,000 profit on bitcoin but lose $2,000 on ethereum, you only owe taxes on the net gain of $3,000.

Examples of tax strategies for crypto investors

1. **Tax-loss harvesting:**

   this strategy involves selling cryptocurrencies at a loss to offset gains from other investments, reducing your overall tax liability.

   o *Example:* if your portfolio includes a $2,000 gain on bitcoin and a $1,000 loss on solana, selling the solana reduces your taxable gain to $1,000.

2. **Holding for long-term gains:**

   many countries offer lower tax rates for long-term capital gains compared to short-term gains. By holding your cryptocurrency for more than a year, you could significantly reduce your tax bill.

- *Example (us):*

    - Short-term gains (held <1 year) are taxed at your regular income rate.

    - Long-term gains (held >1 year) are taxed at 0%, 15%, or 20%, depending on your income level.

3. **Using tax-free accounts:**

in some jurisdictions, you can invest in crypto through tax-advantaged accounts.

- *Example (canada):* investing in bitcoin etfs through a tax-free savings account (tfsa) allows you to grow your investment without incurring taxes.

4. **Donating crypto:**

donating cryptocurrency to a registered charity can provide tax benefits, including deducting the donation's fair market value from your taxable income.

- *Example:* if you donate $10,000 worth of bitcoin, you may be eligible for a $10,000 tax deduction while avoiding capital gains taxes.

5. **Relocating to crypto-friendly jurisdictions:**

   some countries have no or low taxes on crypto gains. While this strategy isn't practical for everyone, it's worth considering for high-net-worth individuals.

   - *Examples:*
     - **Portugal:** no taxes on crypto trading for individuals.
     - **Dubai:** a tax-free haven for cryptocurrency investors.

Final thoughts

Regulation and taxation are unavoidable aspects of cryptocurrency investing, but they don't have to be overwhelming. By staying informed about global regulations and proactively managing your tax obligations, you can protect your investments and ensure compliance. Remember, knowledge is your best defense—keep meticulous records, consult with professionals when needed, and leverage strategies to minimize your tax burden while maximizing your returns. In the ever-changing world of crypto, preparation is key to navigating the regulatory landscape with confidence.

10 CHANGE

How Crypto is Changing Industries

Cryptocurrency is far more than just an investment opportunity—it's a transformative force reshaping industries around the globe. From revolutionizing traditional finance to enabling new ways of owning digital assets, crypto is at the forefront of innovation. In this chapter, we'll explore how decentralized finance (defi), non-fungible tokens (nfts), and the metaverse are disrupting existing systems and creating new opportunities. We'll also highlight success stories that illustrate crypto's real-world impact.

Defi (Decentralized Finance): Replacing Traditional Banks

Decentralized Finance, or defi, is one of the most groundbreaking applications of cryptocurrency. It replaces traditional financial systems like banks, lenders, and payment processors with decentralized platforms that operate entirely on blockchain technology.

What is defi?

Defi platforms allow users to access financial services—like lending, borrowing, and trading—without intermediaries. Instead of going through a bank, users interact directly with smart contracts on blockchain networks like Ethereum.

How It Works:

- Users deposit cryptocurrency into decentralized applications (dapps), which execute transactions automatically based on pre-set rules.

- These dapps are powered by smart contracts, ensuring transparency, security, and efficiency.

How defi is Changing Finance

1. **Lending and Borrowing:**

    defi platforms like Aave and Compound allow users to lend their cryptocurrency and earn interest or borrow against their holdings without the need for credit checks.

- *Example:* If you own Ethereum but don't want to sell it, you can deposit it into a platform like Aave as collateral and borrow stablecoins like USDC. This lets you access funds while still benefiting from Ethereum's potential price increase.

2. **Yield Farming:**

Users can earn high returns by providing liquidity to decentralized exchanges (dexs) like Uniswap or pancakeswap.

- *Example:* By depositing two assets (e.g., ETH and DAI) into a liquidity pool, you earn a share of the trading fees, generating passive income.

3. **Eliminating Middlemen:**

Traditional banks charge fees and take days to process international payments. Defi enables instant, borderless transactions at a fraction of the cost.

Real-World Impact:

- **In Emerging Markets:** defi is giving millions of unbanked individuals access to financial services. For example, a farmer in rural Africa can now secure a loan using cryptocurrency as collateral, bypassing traditional barriers like lack of credit history.

- **For Businesses:** defi allows companies to access global liquidity without relying on banks, enabling faster and cheaper financing.

Nfts: Art, Gaming, and Ownership Rights

Non-fungible tokens, or nfts, are revolutionizing how we think about ownership in the digital age. Unlike cryptocurrencies like Bitcoin, which are interchangeable, nfts represent unique digital assets that cannot be replaced or replicated.

Nfts in Art

Nfts have given digital artists a new way to monetize their work. By minting their art as nfts on platforms like opensea or Rarible, creators can sell directly to collectors without relying on galleries or intermediaries.

Why It Matters:

- **Provenance and Royalties:** Blockchain technology ensures that the authenticity and ownership history of the artwork are publicly verifiable. Artists can also program royalties into the NFT, earning a percentage every time their work is resold.

- *Example:* Digital artist Beeple made headlines in 2021 when his NFT piece, *Everydays: The First 5000 Days*, sold for $69 million at auction.

Nfts in Gaming

Nfts are transforming the gaming industry by allowing players to truly own in-game items, characters, and assets. These items can be traded or sold outside the game, creating real-world value.

Example:

- **Axie Infinity:** This blockchain-based game lets players earn cryptocurrency by breeding and battling virtual creatures (nfts called Axies). Some players in countries like the Philippines have even made a full-time income from the game.

Nfts in Real Estate and Music

- **Virtual Real Estate:** Platforms like Decentraland and The Sandbox allow users to buy, sell, and develop virtual land as nfts. These properties are used for hosting events, advertising, or even building virtual businesses.

- **Music:** Musicians are using nfts to sell albums, concert tickets, and exclusive content directly to fans.

    - *Example:* Kings of Leon became the first major band to release an album as an NFT, generating over $2 million in sales.

The Metaverse: Cryptocurrency in Virtual Worlds

The metaverse is an immersive digital universe where users interact, socialize, and conduct business using avatars. Cryptocurrencies and blockchain technology are integral to this ecosystem, enabling decentralized ownership and commerce.

How Crypto Powers the Metaverse

1. **Virtual Economies:**

    Cryptocurrencies like Decentraland's MANA and The Sandbox's SAND serve as the currencies for their respective virtual worlds. Users can buy virtual land, clothing for their avatars, and even digital art.

2. **Decentralized Ownership**

    In the metaverse, assets like land and goods are represented as nfts. This ensures users have true ownership and the ability to transfer or sell their assets outside the platform.

3. **Real-World Integration:**

    Major brands are entering the metaverse to market their products and services.

    - *Example:* Gucci launched a virtual collection in Roblox, while Adidas collaborated with NFT creators to release exclusive digital sneakers.

Success Stories

While crypto's transformative potential is clear, real-world success stories illustrate its tangible impact.

Tesla and Bitcoin

Tesla made waves in 2021 when it announced a $1.5 billion investment in Bitcoin. The company also briefly accepted Bitcoin as payment for its vehicles, highlighting the growing adoption of crypto by mainstream businesses.

Why It Matters:

- Tesla's move legitimized Bitcoin as a corporate treasury asset, encouraging other companies like microstrategy to follow suit.

- The announcement contributed to Bitcoin's price surge, demonstrating how institutional adoption drives market growth.

El Salvador's Bitcoin Adoption

El Salvador became the first country in the world to adopt Bitcoin as legal tender in 2021. The government launched the **Chivo Wallet**, providing citizens with $30 worth of Bitcoin to encourage usage.

Impact on the Economy:

- **Remittances:** With Bitcoin, Salvadorans can send and receive remittances without paying high fees to traditional money transfer services like Western Union.

    Tourism and Investment: Bitcoin adoption attracted crypto enthusiasts and investors, boosting the country's economy.

Example:

In rural areas, small businesses began accepting Bitcoin payments, empowering unbanked populations and integrating them into the global economy.

Final Thoughts

Cryptocurrency is no longer just a speculative asset—it's a transformative technology reshaping industries, creating new markets, and empowering individuals worldwide. Whether it's through defi's challenge to traditional finance, nfts' redefinition of digital ownership, or the metaverse's creation of virtual economies, crypto is laying the foundation for the future. These success stories are just the beginning of what's possible in a world driven by blockchain innovation.

CHAPTER 11: EMERGING TRENDS

The cryptocurrency space thrives on innovation, with new technologies and trends emerging rapidly to address challenges and expand possibilities. As the industry matures, its impact is poised to extend far beyond financial markets, touching on how we interact with the internet, conduct transactions, and tackle global sustainability issues. In this chapter, we'll explore the most exciting trends shaping the future of crypto—Web 3.0, Layer 2 solutions, and green cryptocurrencies—while highlighting key risks to watch, such as security challenges, quantum computing, and market saturation.

The Next Big Things

Web 3.0: Decentralizing the Internet

Web 3.0 is often described as the next evolution of the internet—a decentralized version that gives users control over their data, interactions, and digital assets. Unlike the current Web 2.0 era, dominated by centralized tech giants like Google, Facebook, and Amazon, Web 3.0 leverages blockchain technology to create a more open, user-centric internet.

Key Features of Web 3.0:

1. **Decentralization:**

   Data and applications are distributed across blockchain networks, reducing reliance on centralized servers and corporations. This eliminates single points of failure and fosters greater transparency.

2. **User Ownership:**

   Through cryptocurrencies and tokens, users can own a stake in the platforms they interact with, participating in governance and sharing in the platform's success.

3. **Interoperability:**

Web 3.0 applications (dapps) are built to work seamlessly across different platforms and blockchains, creating a more connected digital ecosystem.

Examples of Web 3.0 Projects:

- **Filecoin (FIL):** A decentralized storage network that allows users to rent out unused storage space, creating a global peer-to-peer marketplace for data storage.

- **Brave Browser and Basic Attention Token (BAT):** Brave reimagines online advertising by rewarding users for their attention in BAT tokens, flipping the traditional model where corporations profit from user data.

- **Ethereum Name Service (ENS):** Simplifies blockchain addresses by allowing users to register human-readable names (e.g., alice.eth), making cryptocurrency wallets and dapps more accessible.

-

Impact of Web 3.0:

Imagine an internet where you control your personal data, interact with decentralized social networks, and earn rewards for the value you create—all without sacrificing privacy. Web 3.0 promises to democratize the internet, empowering individuals while reducing the influence of centralized corporations.

Layer 2 Solutions: Improving Scalability

Scalability remains a critical challenge for blockchain networks like Ethereum and Bitcoin. As adoption grows, these networks often struggle to handle the volume of transactions, leading to high fees and slow processing times. **Layer 2 solutions** address this issue by building on top of existing blockchains to improve speed, reduce costs, and enhance user experience.

How Layer 2 Works:

Layer 2 solutions process transactions off the main blockchain (Layer 1) and record the final results back on the main chain. This reduces congestion and improves overall efficiency.

Examples of Layer 2 Solutions:

- **Polygon (MATIC):** A popular Layer 2 solution for Ethereum, Polygon enables faster and cheaper transactions while maintaining Ethereum's security.

- **Lightning Network:** A Layer 2 protocol for Bitcoin that allows instant micropayments by creating off-chain payment channels.

- **Arbitrum and Optimism:** Rollup solutions that bundle multiple transactions into a single batch, significantly reducing gas fees on Ethereum.

Real-World Applications:

- Defi platforms like Uniswap and Aave integrate Layer 2 solutions to provide seamless, low-cost services to users.

- NFT marketplaces like opensea explore Layer 2 options to reduce minting costs for creators and traders.

Why Layer 2 Matters:

Scalability is essential for mass adoption. Without Layer 2 solutions, blockchain networks risk being too slow and expensive to compete with traditional systems. By enhancing speed and affordability, Layer 2 technologies are paving the way for blockchain to become a mainstream tool.

Green Cryptocurrencies: Sustainable Blockchain Solutions

Cryptocurrency has faced criticism for its environmental impact, particularly in the case of energy-intensive Proof-of-Work (pow) mining. In response, the industry is evolving to embrace sustainability, with new projects and technologies designed to minimize carbon footprints.

Innovations in Green Cryptocurrencies:

1. **Proof-of-Stake (pos):** pos replaces mining with staking, drastically reducing energy consumption.

Ethereum's transition to pos in 2022 reduced its energy usage by over 99%.

2. **Eco-Friendly Blockchains:** Projects like Algorand and Tezos are designed to be energy-efficient, using minimal computational resources for validation.

3. **Renewable Energy Mining:** Mining operations increasingly adopt renewable energy sources like hydro, wind, and solar to power their activities.

Examples of Green Cryptocurrencies:

- **Chia (XCH):** Utilizes a "proof-of-space-and-time" consensus mechanism, relying on unused hard drive space rather than energy-intensive mining.

- **Nano (NANO):** A lightweight cryptocurrency that uses minimal energy, offering instant and fee-free transactions.

- **Celo (CELO):** Focused on sustainability and accessibility, Celo uses a lightweight protocol optimized for mobile devices.

Why Green Cryptocurrencies Matter: As climate concerns grow, sustainability will become a key differentiator for blockchain projects. By reducing environmental impact, green cryptocurrencies not only address ethical concerns but also position themselves for broader adoption in a climate-conscious world.

Risks to Watch

While emerging trends hold immense promise, several risks could undermine the growth and stability of the cryptocurrency industry. Understanding these challenges is crucial for navigating the road ahead.

Security Challenges

Blockchain networks are inherently secure, but vulnerabilities in smart contracts, exchanges, and wallets can still lead to significant losses.

1. **Hacks and Exploits:** Cyberattacks targeting defi platforms and exchanges have resulted in billions of dollars in losses.

    - *Example:* In 2021, the Poly Network hack exposed vulnerabilities in smart contracts, leading to a $600 million theft (later partially recovered).

2. **Phishing Attacks:** Scammers often use fake websites or emails to steal users' private keys and funds.

    - *Example:* An investor clicks a link in a fraudulent email, thinking it's from their wallet provider, and unknowingly shares their private key.

How to Mitigate Security Risks:

- Use hardware wallets for secure storage.
- Verify urls and avoid clicking on unverified links.
- Choose platforms with strong security measures and insurance.

Quantum Computing

Quantum computing poses a theoretical threat to blockchain security by potentially breaking the cryptographic algorithms that protect blockchain networks.

1. **Why It's a Concern**

   Traditional cryptographic methods rely on problems that are computationally infeasible for current computers to solve. However, quantum computers could solve these problems exponentially faster.

2. **Industry Response:**

   Developers are already exploring quantum-resistant cryptographic algorithms to future-proof blockchain systems.

   - *Example:* Algorand has initiated research into post-quantum security measures.

Market Saturation

The explosive growth of cryptocurrency has led to a crowded market, with thousands of projects vying for attention. While this fosters innovation, it also creates challenges.

1. **Scams and Low-Quality Projects:** Many tokens lack real utility or innovation, leading to wasted investments.

    o *Example:* The Squid Game Token scam in 2021 defrauded investors by exploiting a popular TV show's name.

2. **Investor Fatigue:** With so many options, truly valuable projects may struggle to stand out.

How to Avoid Saturation Risks:

- Focus on projects with clear use cases, strong development teams, and active communities.

- Conduct thorough research before investing in new tokens.

Final Thoughts

The future of cryptocurrency is rich with potential. Emerging trends like Web 3.0, Layer 2 solutions, and green cryptocurrencies are addressing critical challenges and paving the way for mass adoption. However, risks such as security vulnerabilities, quantum computing, and market saturation cannot be ignored. By staying informed and adopting a cautious, forward-looking approach, investors and developers alike can thrive in this dynamic and rapidly evolving industry. The crypto journey is just beginning, and the opportunities are as vast as the challenges.

CHAPTER 12: BECOMING A SAVVY CRYPTO INVESTOR

Becoming a savvy crypto investor requires more than just knowing when to buy or sell. It's about cultivating a mindset of continuous learning, building a robust strategy, and staying grounded during market volatility. In this chapter, we'll explore how to stay informed with reliable sources, the importance of networking with the crypto community, and tips for developing a long-term investment strategy that can withstand the ups and downs of this dynamic market.

Staying informed

Cryptocurrency markets move at lightning speed, with new developments happening daily. Staying updated is critical for making informed decisions, but separating valuable information from noise can be challenging.

Trusted sources for crypto news and updates

The crypto space is filled with rumors, hype, and misinformation. To avoid falling victim to false narratives, rely on reputable sources for your information.

1. **News websites and blogs:**

    - **Coindesk:** a leading source for crypto news, analysis, and market trends.

    - **The block:** focuses on research-driven insights and breaking news.

    - **Decrypt:** offers beginner-friendly explanations alongside industry news.

2. **Data platforms:**

    - **Coinmarketcap and coingecko:** track market prices, trading volumes, and rankings for thousands of cryptocurrencies.

- **Glassnode and intotheblock:** provide on-chain analytics to help you understand market trends and investor behavior.

3. **Social media and forums:**

    - Follow thought leaders like vitalik buterin (ethereum founder) or balaji srinivasan (crypto futurist) on twitter.

    - Join forums like reddit's **r/cryptocurrency** for discussions, but be cautious of hype-driven posts.

4. **Official project channels:**

    - Many crypto projects maintain active communication via twitter, telegram, and discord. These platforms are excellent for getting updates straight from the source.

    - *Example:* if you're invested in solana, following their official twitter handle ensures you get timely information about network upgrades or issues.

Networking with the crypto community
The crypto community is one of the most active and supportive ecosystems in the financial world. Engaging with this community can provide valuable insights, early access to opportunities, and even collaborative learning.

1. **Join online communities:**

   - Participate in telegram or discord groups for specific projects you're interested in. These are often hubs for real-time discussions and updates.

   - *Example:* if you're exploring decentralized finance (defi), joining communities like aave's discord can help you understand the platform better.

2. **Attend meetups and conferences:**

   - Events like **bitcoin miami** or **ethglobal** provide networking opportunities with developers, investors, and industry leaders.

   - *Example:* a casual conversation at a conference might lead to discovering a promising startup before it gains mainstream attention.

3. **Collaborate with peers:**

    o   Building relationships with other investors allows you to share research, debate strategies, and learn from each other's experiences.

Pro tip: always approach community insights with a critical mind. While many members are knowledgeable, some may spread misinformation or promote low-quality projects for personal gain.

Your long-term strategy

The crypto market is notoriously volatile, with prices often swinging wildly in short periods. Developing a clear, long-term strategy helps you stay focused on your goals and avoid emotional decisions.

Adapting to a rapidly changing landscape

The only constant in crypto is change. Technology evolves, regulations shift, and market sentiment fluctuates. A savvy investor must remain adaptable while staying grounded in long-term

goals.
1. **Diversification is key:**

    don't put all your eggs in one basket. Spread your investments across various cryptocurrencies, sectors (e.g., defi, nfts, layer 1 blockchains), and risk levels.

    - *Example:* your portfolio might include blue-chip cryptocurrencies like bitcoin and ethereum, a few promising altcoins like solana or chainlink, and stablecoins for liquidity.

2. **Reassess your portfolio regularly:**

    as the market evolves, some projects may lose relevance while others gain traction. Periodically review your investments to ensure they align with your strategy.

    - *Example:* if a project fails to deliver on its roadmap or loses its competitive edge, consider reallocating funds to stronger performers.

3. **Stay ahead of trends:**

    keep an eye on emerging technologies and industries within the crypto space, such as web 3.0 or green cryptocurrencies.

    - *Example:* early adopters of defi platforms like aave and uniswap reaped substantial rewards as these projects became mainstream.

Keeping your emotions in check during market turbulence

One of the most challenging aspects of crypto investing is managing emotions. Fear and greed are powerful forces that can lead to impulsive decisions, such as panic-selling during a dip or buying into a hype-driven rally at the top.

1. **Stick to your plan:**

    define your investment goals, risk tolerance, and exit strategy before entering the market. When emotions run high, refer back to your plan.

    - *Example:* if your goal is to hold bitcoin for five years, don't let a 20% drop tempt you into selling prematurely.

2. **Use dollar-cost averaging (dca):**

   investing a fixed amount at regular intervals smooths out the effects of market volatility, reducing the urge to time the market.

   - *Example:* instead of investing $5,000 in ethereum all at once, invest $500 monthly over ten months.

3. **Avoid fomo (fear of missing out):** crypto is full of stories about people making life-changing gains overnight, but chasing the next big thing often leads to losses.

   - *Example:* during the 2021 bull run, many bought into dogecoin at its peak due to fomo, only to see its price crash shortly after.

4. **Stay calm during dips:**

   crypto corrections are common and often temporary. Viewing them as opportunities to buy rather than reasons to panic can shift your perspective.

- *Example:* when bitcoin dropped from $69,000 to $16,000 in 2022, patient investors who bought during the dip saw significant gains in the recovery.

Pro tip: if market turbulence is causing stress, step back and remind yourself of your long-term goals. Avoid checking prices obsessively, as this can amplify anxiety.

Final thoughts

Becoming a savvy crypto investor is not about predicting every market movement but about staying informed, building meaningful connections, and sticking to a well-thought-out strategy. By engaging with trusted sources, networking with the community, and managing your emotions during volatility, you'll be better equipped to navigate the dynamic world of cryptocurrency. Remember, the most successful investors are those who combine knowledge with patience, adaptability, and a clear vision for the future.

CHAPTER 13 CONCLUSION

The cryptocurrency world can feel overwhelming, especially when you're just starting out. But as we've explored throughout this book, it's also full of opportunities for those willing to learn, take calculated risks, and embrace its potential. Let's conclude by revisiting the key insights you've gained and looking at the bigger picture of how cryptocurrency can fit into your broader financial journey.

Taking the first step
One of the most important lessons in cryptocurrency investing is to start small and stay informed. You don't need to dive in headfirst or risk more than you can afford to lose. The key is taking that first step, learning as you go, and growing your confidence over time.

Recap of key insights

1. **Understand the basics before investing:**

    familiarize yourself with the concepts of blockchain, cryptocurrency types, and how markets operate. Knowledge is your greatest asset.

    o *Example:* before investing in ethereum, understand its use cases, like smart contracts and decentralized apps, which give it value beyond being a digital currency.

2. **Choose your investments wisely:**

   start with established cryptocurrencies like bitcoin or ethereum before exploring riskier altcoins. Diversify your portfolio to balance potential rewards with manageable risks.

   o *Example:* allocating 70% of your initial investment to blue-chip coins and 30% to promising altcoins reduces your exposure to volatility.

3. **Security is paramount:** use trusted exchanges, secure your assets in wallets (preferably hardware wallets), and safeguard your private keys. Losing access to your wallet can mean losing your investment permanently.

   o *Example:* store your seed phrases offline in a safe location to prevent unauthorized access.

4. **Have a strategy and stick to it:** whether you're hodling for the long term, trading short term, or staking for passive income, a clear strategy keeps you grounded during market turbulence.

- *Example:* dollar-cost averaging into bitcoin reduces the impact of short-term volatility while building your position over time.

5. **Learn to navigate risks:** be aware of scams, market sentiment, and emotional trading. Cryptocurrency is an exciting but volatile space, so staying level-headed is crucial.

    - *Example:* if a coin promises guaranteed returns of 50% apy, question its legitimacy and do thorough research.

Encouragement to start small

Starting small doesn't mean starting insignificantly. Even a modest investment can teach you valuable lessons about how markets work, how to manage your emotions, and how to refine your strategy

Examples of starting small:

- Invest $50 or $100 in a cryptocurrency you've researched. Use this as an opportunity to practice buying, storing, and tracking your assets.

- Stake a small amount of cryptocurrency, like 10 ada, to see how staking works and earn passive rewards.

- Explore a decentralized finance (defi) platform with a tiny deposit to understand how lending, borrowing, or yield farming operates.

Pro tip: starting small minimizes risk while building your knowledge and confidence. As you grow more comfortable, you can gradually scale up your investments.

The bigger picture
Cryptocurrency is not a standalone investment. It's a powerful tool that can complement traditional assets in a well-diversified portfolio. By understanding its role in the bigger picture of personal finance, you can use crypto to enhance your financial future without overexposing yourself to unnecessary risk.

Cryptocurrency as part of a diversified financial future

1. **Balancing traditional and modern investments:**

   while crypto offers high growth potential, it also carries higher risks. Balancing crypto with traditional investments like stocks, bonds, and real estate can provide stability and reduce volatility in your overall portfolio.

   - *Example:* a balanced portfolio might consist of 60% traditional assets, 30% cryptocurrency, and 10% alternative investments like gold or art.

2. **Hedging against inflation:**

cryptocurrencies like bitcoin are often considered "digital gold" because of their limited supply and potential to act as a hedge against inflation.

- *Example:* as fiat currencies lose value due to inflation, bitcoin's scarcity could make it a store of value, much like gold.

3. **Exploring new opportunities:**

beyond investment, cryptocurrency opens doors to participate in emerging technologies like decentralized finance (defi), non-fungible tokens (nfts), and the metaverse. These areas could shape the future of how we interact with money, art, and virtual environments.

- *Example:* owning virtual land in a blockchain-based metaverse like decentraland could yield returns as brands and businesses invest in digital real estate.

A new paradigm for financial independence

Cryptocurrency represents more than just a financial opportunity—it embodies a shift in how individuals interact with wealth, technology, and global markets. By participating in this space, you're joining a movement that empowers individuals, decentralizes power, and democratizes access to financial tools.

The bigger message:

- Crypto allows you to take control of your financial future in ways traditional systems often don't.

- Whether it's enabling unbanked populations to access financial services or giving artists a new way to monetize their work, cryptocurrency is about breaking barriers and creating opportunities.

Final encouragement

As you close this book, remember that every great journey begins with a single step. The world of cryptocurrency can be intimidating at first, but with knowledge, patience, and a willingness to learn, you can navigate it successfully. Start small, stay informed, and never stop asking questions. Cryptocurrency isn't just a trend—it's a tool for building a diversified, forward-thinking financial future.

The possibilities are endless, and your journey is just beginning. Take that first step and embrace the future of finance with confidence. You're now equipped to succeed—one informed decision at a time.

ABOUT THE AUTHOR

Arthur Crandon is a retired lawyer and a prolific writer. He is British and grew up in a rural community in Somerset. Recently, he has been acknowledges as a prominent Political Commentator

He has lived in England, Wales, Hong Kong and the Philippines and now spends most of his time in the Philippines with his Visayan wife and their son.

He loves to hear from anyone who has anything to do with the Philippines – you can email him anytime on:

ac@arthurcrandon.co.uk

Crypto Clarity: Demystifying Cryptocurrency for Everyday Investors

Copyright Arthur Crandon 2024

All rights reserved. No part of this book may be reproduced, stored in a retrieval system, or transmitted in any form or by any means—electronic, mechanical, photocopying, recording, or otherwise—without the prior written permission of the publisher, except for brief quotations in critical reviews or articles.

This is a work of fiction. Names, characters, places, and incidents are either the product of the author's imagination or used fictitiously. Any resemblance to actual persons, living or dead,

ISBN: 9798304404853

Cover design by Lynnie Ceniza

Interior design and formatting by Lynnie Ceniza

Published by Arthur Crandon Publishing

Visit our website: Arthurcrandon.co.uk

DISCLAIMER

The information provided in this book is for general informational purposes only. It does not constitute legal, financial, or professional advice. While every effort has been made to ensure accuracy, the author and publisher assume no responsibility for errors or omissions. Readers should consult with appropriate professionals for specific advice tailored to their individual circumstances.

First Edition: August 2024

If you enjoyed this book, please consider leaving a review – your feedback may help others to discover the book.

If you send me a screenshot of your review, I will send you a copy of another of my Self-Help books.

You can email me on ac@arthurcrandon.co.uk

To leave a review – just go back to the book on Amazon and scroll down – the link to leave a review is on the left hand side.

Thanks, and very best wishes.